CAREERS FOR
HEROES

MOUNTED

AND

CANINE POLICE

Lee Fitzgerald

PowerKiDS
press.

New York

Published in 2016 by The Rosen Publishing Group, Inc.
29 East 21st Street, New York, NY 10010

First Edition

Editor: Katie Kawa
Book Design: Mickey Harmon

Photo Credits: Cover (man in foreground) John Roman Images/Shutterstock.com; cover (background) Leonard Zhukovsky/Shutterstock.com; cover, pp. 1, 3, 4, 6, 8, 10, 12–13, 14, 16, 18, 20, 22–24 (gray and yellow textures) siro46/Shutterstock.com; p. 4 Rob Hainer/Shutterstock.com; p. 5 Stuart Monk/Shutterstock.com; p. 7 Paul McKinnon/Shutterstock.com; p. 9 Charles Rex Arbogast/AP Images; p. 11 Frank Gaertner/Shutterstock.com; p. 13 CristinaMuraca/Shutterstock.com; pp. 15, 22 a katz/Shutterstock.com; p. 17 bikeriderlondon/Shutterstock.com; p. 19 Jeff T. Green/Stringer/Getty Images News/Getty Images; p. 21 GABRIEL BOUYS/Staff/AFP/Getty Images.

Cataloging-in-Publication Data

Fitzgerald, Lee.
Mounted and canine police / by Lee Fitzgerald.
p. cm. — (Careers for heroes)
Includes index.
ISBN 978-1-5081-4384-0 (pbk.)
ISBN 978-1-4994-1860-6 (6-pack)
ISBN 978-1-5081-4385-7 (library binding)
1. Mounted police — Juvenile literature. 2. Police horses — Juvenile literature. 3. Police dogs — Juvenile literature. I. Fitzgerald, Lee. II. Title.
HV7922.F58 2016
363.2'32—d23

Manufactured in the United States of America

CPSIA Compliance Information: Batch #BW16PK: For Further Information contact Rosen Publishing, New York, New York at 1-800-237-9932

CONTENTS

WORKING WITH ANIMALS

Police officers work hard every day to keep people in their community safe. The work they do can be very dangerous, or unsafe. Police officers often have partners, or people they work with, so they don't have to go into dangerous **situations** alone.

Sometimes a police officer's partner isn't another person—it's an animal! Mounted police officers ride horses as they work. Canine **units**, which are commonly called K-9 units, are special police teams that use dogs to help solve crimes. If you like working with animals and helping people, one of these exciting jobs might be a good fit for you.

FAST FACT!

K-9 units have that name because "K-9" sounds like "canine," which is another word for "dog."

Both the police officers and animals in mounted and canine police units go through many hours of training before they officially begin working together.

HEROES ON HORSEBACK

Mounted police units are part of police departments throughout the United States. Mounted police are generally found in larger cities, such as Chicago, Houston, and New York City. The New York Police Department's mounted police unit is one of the largest in the country, with about 75 officers and 60 horses.

Mounted police officers play an important part in both public safety and **public relations**. Because people like horses, many mounted police officers are asked to visit schools and other groups for **demonstrations**. These officers must be friendly and have good public speaking skills.

FAST FACT!

Horses and officers are carefully chosen to be part of mounted police units in the United States and around the world.

The Royal Canadian Mounted Police is Canada's national police force. It got its name from the horses once used to get officers from place to place. Now, they use horses as part of a group called the Musical Ride that can be seen at special events in Canada and around the world.

CONTROLLING CROWDS

Mounted police officers are easy to spot in a crowd, and that's exactly what they want. Being on horseback allows them to be higher than everyone around them. This gives them a wider view of a crowd. For this reason, mounted police officers are often used in places where crowds are common, such as Times Square in New York City and Michigan Avenue in Chicago.

Being on horseback allows officers to easily see crowds, and it allows people in crowds to easily see officers. This can deter, or stop, people from committing a crime. Also, if a person needs help, they can easily find a mounted officer.

FAST FACT!

It's been said that one mounted police officer is as **effective** as 10 to 12 officers on the ground in a crowd.

Mounted police officers can travel in areas that would be hard to get through on foot or by car.

TOUGH TRAINING

Because mounted police officers spend so much time in crowd-control situations, they should be comfortable in crowds. They should also be comfortable around horses. If you're good with animals and interested in being a police officer, this might be a good career for you.

Officers and horses train for long periods of time before they join a mounted police unit. For example, the training period in Chicago is 14 weeks. Mounted police officers and horses then go through further training throughout their careers. This allows the officers and horses to be at their best whenever they're on the job.

FAST FACT!

Most police horses are geldings—male horses that can't make babies with a female horse. Geldings are generally calmer than other male horses.

Mounted police officers wear a helmet to **protect** their head in case they ever fall off their horse.

LOOK UP FOR HELP!

People are taught from a young age to find a police officer if they need help or see something dangerous happening. Mounted police officers are easy to find, which makes them good people to look for in a crisis, or dangerous situation.

Where are mounted police found?

1	places visited by many travelers (Times Square)
2	Super Bowl events
3	parades
4	parks (Chicago's Lincoln Park)
5	Major League Baseball World Series games
6	protests in crowded areas

These are just some of the many events and places throughout the United States where you can find mounted police hard at work keeping the peace.

In May 2010, two people saw what turned out to be a car **bomb** in Times Square. They spotted two mounted police officers above the crowd and told them what they saw. Those officers then cleared the area so members of the bomb squad could safely do their job. No one was hurt, and the bomb was destroyed.

FAST FACT!

Mounted police are often used to control crowds during major sporting events, such as the National Football League's Super Bowl.

DOGS ON THE FORCE

Dogs are another common animal used by police departments around the world. K-9 units make good use of dogs' strong sense of smell. The dogs are trained to find things and people using that sense, which is much stronger than a person's sense of smell.

Each dog in a K-9 unit has its own handler, or an officer chosen to work with and care for that dog. The dog lives with its police handler and their family. It's the handler's job to feed and care for the dog. They also help the dog stay fit by taking them on walks or jogs.

FAST FACT!

The most common kind of dog used by police departments is the German shepherd. German shepherds are smart, strong dogs with a good sense of smell. They also like being around people.

Police officers often form a strong bond with their police dog because they spend much of their time together.

SNIFFING OUT CRIME

Not all K-9 dogs are trained to do the same job. Many K-9 dogs are trained to find missing people using their sense of smell. They often smell something that belonged to the person. Then, they track that scent until they find who they're looking for. Dogs are an important part of search-and-rescue teams around the world.

Other police dogs are trained to find illegal drugs using their sense of smell. They can also be trained to find explosives, such as bombs. A police dog and its handler often work long hours, and they're sometimes put in dangerous situations.

FAST FACT!

K-9 dogs and their handlers often visit schools or other public places to show people what they do. They're a popular part of police departments throughout the United States.

Police dogs generally work for five to seven years.
They have a hard job!

TRAINING TOGETHER

In order to be a police dog's handler, an officer needs to be good with animals. They should also be friendly and comfortable talking to a crowd. This is important because police dogs and their handlers spend a lot of time interacting with the public.

Police dogs and their handlers go through weeks of training together in order to become a good team. Handlers need to be open-minded people who are ready to try different training methods when one doesn't seem to be working. If you have these qualities, then you might make a good K-9 handler.

FAST FACT!

Police dogs and their handlers are often called in to help with **stressful** situations. Handlers need to be able to stay calm in order to keep their dog calm and **focused**.

Training doesn't stop after a dog joins the police force. The dog and its handler continue to train together to keep the dog's senses sharp.

TRAKR'S STORY

Heroic dogs have been helping police forces for hundreds of years. They've saved many lives and helped find dangerous criminals. Police dogs have also found many missing people after natural **disasters** or **terrorist** attacks.

After the terrorist attacks of September 11, 2001, people were buried under what used to be the World Trade Center buildings in New York City. A Canadian police dog named Trakr located the last person to be found alive at the site of the attacks. Trakr's handler, James Symington, drove 15 hours from Nova Scotia, Canada, to help the people of New York City following the events of September 11.

FAST FACT!

Trakr had stopped working as a police dog months before traveling to New York City. However, Symington knew his dog would still be able to help people, so Trakr came along.

Trakr was named one of history's most heroic animals by *Time* magazine.

HEROIC HELPERS

Animals are an important part of police forces around the world. They help keep us safe, and they help create a positive connection between the police and the public.

These heroic animals need heroic people to work with and care for them. If you're interested in becoming part of one of these units, continue to learn more about them. You might even see a demonstration by one of these units in your city or town. Maybe one day you'll be a mounted or K-9 police officer, teaching people about the heroic things you and your animal partner do!

GLOSSARY

bomb: A device made to explode under certain conditions in order to hurt people or destroy property.

demonstration: An act of showing someone how something is done.

disaster: Something that happens suddenly and causes loss and suffering for many people.

effective: Producing a wanted result.

focused: Having one's attention directed at something specific.

protect: To keep safe.

public relations: The job of telling people things about a person or group in order to have the public see that person or group in a positive way.

situation: All the facts, conditions, and events that affect someone or something in a certain time and place.

stressful: Causing strong feelings of worry.

terrorist: A person who uses violence to scare people as a way of achieving a political goal.

unit: A single thing, person, or group that is part of something larger.

INDEX

WEBSITES

Due to the changing nature of Internet links, PowerKids Press has developed an online list of websites related to the subject of this book. This site is updated regularly. Please use this link to access the list: www.powerkidslinks.com/chero/mcp